Don't Leave Money on the Table

Maximizing Social Security and Medicare Benefits: A Guide for Financial Advisors

Michael Soos

Don't Leave Money on the Table

Independently Published

Copyright © 2023, Michael Soos

Published in the United States of America

230526-02326.2.2

ISBN: 9798858032434

Here's What's Inside...

Foreword

I have had the pleasure of working with Michael Soos, whose Social Security and Medicare expertise has been invaluable to me and my clients. As a consultant in my financial planning practice, Michael has consistently demonstrated exceptional knowledge and dedication, making him an indispensable asset to our team. Navigating the intricate landscape of Social Security and Medicare can often be overwhelming, but Michael's guidance has made the process remarkably smooth and stress-free. His deep understanding of the complexities and ability to translate these intricate concepts into simple, comprehensible terms sets him apart as an exceptional professional.

What I admire most about Michael is his genuine passion for helping others. He goes above and beyond to ensure that each client receives personalized attention and tailored solutions that align with their unique financial goals and circumstances. His patience and attentiveness create a supportive environment where clients feel comfortable asking questions and seeking clarification on complex matters. Michael's ability to analyze intricate financial scenarios and provide strategic recommendations is impressive. His expertise in maximizing Social Security benefits and optimizing Medicare coverage has consistently yielded outstanding results for my clients. Whether devising a comprehensive retirement plan or navigating the intricacies of healthcare costs, Michael's insights have proven invaluable repeatedly. Beyond his technical prowess, Michael possesses exceptional interpersonal skills. He is a consummate professional who is always approachable, responsive, and empathetic. His ability to establish a strong rapport with clients fosters trust and confidence, enabling them to make informed decisions with peace of mind.

Michael's book on Social Security and Medicare is a game-changer for anyone seeking clarity in this often-convoluted realm. His knack for simplifying complex topics will undoubtedly empower readers to make informed choices and secure their financial future.

His contributions have had a profound impact on my financial planning practice and the lives of our clients.

Joe Silva

Financial Planner
Blue Ridge Financial Planning
Fort Mill, SC

Introduction

Are your clients coming in asking about Social Security and Medicare benefits? It's complicated, isn't it? Not only because something has changed every time we turn about, but everyone has a different issue to consider. Social Security and Medicare benefits are ever-changing and require due consideration because of the individual's specific issues.

Thirty years ago, my father wanted to retire early at age 63. The issue was that no one was around to help him with Social Security and Medicare. That issue is still prevalent today, but now, it's more complicated.

I recently helped a financial advisor with a couple retiring early. The husband was 60 years old, and the wife was 61 years old. He retired early with his company buy-out but remained a consultant working several days a week, making $60,000. The wife was a retired schoolteacher. They would take Social Security early at age 62 to supplement their retirement.

By sharing several strategies with them and their advisor, I saved them approximately $20,000 a year in lost benefits. In addition, we were able to help them maximize their future Social Security benefits and lower some of their Medicare costs.

So, What's That Got to Do with You?

This book is to help financial advisors provide their clients with a comprehensive overview of Social Security and Medicare programs. The information in this book is designed to show how your client's choices could impact their retirement planning. It helps you provide practical guidance and strategies to help your clients make informed decisions about their benefits and coverage.

This book helps you understand that taking Social Security is more complex than you think. The goal of maximizing or preserving client benefits takes forethought, planning, and often collaboration. No one wants to leave money on the table when collecting money you have already paid into the system. It is essential to help your clients understand that managing their healthcare costs in retirement can be challenging without guidance. This is especially true if they want to control and keep as much of their Social Security and Medicare benefits as possible.

I am here to help you save yourself and your clients the stress when making those important life-changing decisions.

Here to help you help your clients,

Michael Soos,

Social Security and Medicare Solutions Strategist

Chapter One
Understanding Social Security Benefits

When it comes to Social Security benefits, most clients believe two things.

First, they don't trust the government. Second, they think that Social Security is going broke. I find it interesting when people say that because broke, to me, typically means zero. Social Security is not going broke. The funding of Social Security is a complex and well-debated topic because Social Security is funded through payroll tax. Therefore, during your earning or working years, you are paying payroll tax which funds Social Security. While Social Security is not going broke, that does not mean there are no problems. One of the major issues is that fewer people are working today than 30 years ago. For example, 30 years ago, we had 16 workers for every retiree. Today we have less than three workers per retiree. Therefore, it's not that Social Security is going broke; fewer people are paying payroll tax into the system to fund the ones that are retiring.

More people are retiring than money is coming in to fund the system, and it's not sustainable. The Social Security Administration believes that by 2034 if we continue this trajectory, Social Security will only be able to pay about 78% of the required benefits. Some changes may need to be made to Social Security, but many clients do not understand that the simple fact remains there are only two choices that the government has; reduce benefits or raise taxes over time to compensate for that.

Working Longer and Getting More

Clients need to understand how their benefits are calculated. Working longer and getting more means that the longer you work, typically the more money you will make. The more you pay into the system, the higher your Social Security benefit will be. The opposite also happens as well. Conversely, the fewer years you work, typically the less you make over time and the less your benefits will be.

But I think it's important to understand how benefits are calculated. Social Security uses your highest 35 working years, and without going into much detail, they base it on an average. There is a complicated formula that calculates your benefits, but very simply, they take an average of your 35 highest working years. The first thing you can do to maximize your benefits is make sure you work for 35 years.

Benefits are means tested, and they take the average. This means the first part of your earnings is weighted more heavily than the latter. If you can work, even part-time, that will matter more than having a zero for those early years. If you do not work for 35 years, Social Security puts in a zero for the years you do not have any wages. Those "zero" years may still be part of that 35-year average calculation. That could be very detrimental to individuals in retirement. That is why it is very important to understand how benefits are calculated and how that will affect your benefits over time. It is best to maximize the benefits by working for 35 years. While you cannot always plan your earnings, working a little longer to ensure you meet those 35 years would be best.

Your Earnings Record ▬▬▬▬▬▬▬▬▬▬▬▬▬▬▬▬▬▬▬▬

Years You Worked	Your Taxed Social Security Earnings	Your Taxed Medicare Earnings		Years You Worked	Your Taxed Social Security Earnings	Your Taxed Medicare Earnings
1978	790	790		2009	67,049	67,049
1979	1,362	1,362				
				2010	72,717	72,717
1980	420	420		2011	42,601	42,601
1981	0	0		2012	0	0
1982	1,431	1,431		2013	Not yet recorded	Not yet recorded
1983	11,763	11,763				
1984	7,249	7,249				
1985	8,940	8,940				
1986	7,265	7,265				
1987	7,887	7,887				
1988	0	0				
1989	0	0				
1990	0	0				
1991	0	0				
1992	0	0				
1993	0	0				
1994	0	0				
1995	0	0				
1996	0	0				
1997	0	0				
1998	0	0				
1999	11,917	11,917				
2000	14,430	14,430				

> Zeros are counted in 35- year average

If you have worked fewer than 35 years zeros can lower the average earnings used to calculate your benefit

Calculating... Maximizing... Claiming

A common avoidable surprise I see most people make when claiming their benefits is claiming their benefits too early. What I mean by that is when individuals claim their benefits before they reach their full retirement age. Full retirement age is based on their birth year, with most full retirement ages being 66 or 67. If you claim your benefits before your full retirement age, your monthly benefit amount will be permanently reduced. That could mean a permanent reduction of benefits by 25% or 30% if you take it at 62. Conversely, if you could take it at 66 or 67, your full retirement age, there would not be this reduction. The avoidable surprise I see most people make is claiming their benefits too early. They do this because they do not trust the government, think Social Security is going broke, or think they will not get their benefit and want to take it as early as possible.

They do not realize they are harming themselves and their spouse for future earning years. It could mean a difference of several hundred thousand dollars in lost benefits over time.

Birth Year	Full Retirement Age	Retirement Benefit Reduction at 62
1943 - 1954	66	25.00%
1955	66 & 2 Months	25.83%
1956	66 & 4 Months	26.67%
1957	66 & 6 Months	27.50%
1958	66 & 8 Months	28.33%
1959	66 & 10 Months	29.17%
1960+	67	30.00%

Check Your Employment Record

Another common avoidable surprise most people make regarding their Social Security benefits is not checking their employment records or wages. Social Security allows you, through their website, to go in and open up an account called My Social Security. You can see your wage and earnings records on your Social Security statement. It's important that, at least annually, you go in and check to ensure those records are accurate. Failing to check those can lead to errors in your earnings history, resulting in lower Social Security benefits or earnings.

Social Security does not always call you when there is an error; therefore, you must check your statement for accuracy. If you notice any errors, make sure you bring that to the attention of Social Security. Do what you can to prevent any potential issues so you get the correct amount of Social Security based on your actual earnings.

Earnings Record

Review your earnings history below to ensure it is accurate because we base your future benefits on our record of your earnings. There's a limit to the amount of earnings you pay Social Security taxes on each year. Earnings above the limit do not appear on your earnings record. We have combined your earlier years of earnings below, but you can view your complete earnings record online with *my* Social Security. **If you find an error**, view your full earnings record online and call **1-800-772-1213**.

Work Year	Earnings Taxed for Social Security	Earnings Taxed for Medicare (began 1966)
1981-1990	▬▬	▬▬
1991-2000	▬▬	▬▬
2001-2005	▬▬	▬▬
2006	$0	$0
2007	$0	$0
2008	$0	$0

Chapter Two

Miscalculating Your Full Retirement Age or FRA

DIYers Beware

Whether you are a DIYer or not, the persistent issue is claiming benefits too early. By claiming their benefits too early and not waiting to full retirement age, there are negative consequences. By claiming at full retirement age, you get the full benefits you have paid at full retirement age with no restrictions, penalties, or benefits reductions. For example, if someone claims their benefits at 62 years old instead of waiting until their full retirement age of 66, their benefit will be permanently reduced by 25%. That could mean lost wages or lost benefits of several hundred thousand dollars over that time.

62 vs. 70

I think many people have many different reasons why they might take their benefits at 62 years old. I am generalizing, but it could be because of their health. It could be because they are single and not married. It could be because they do not have longevity in their family. Or it could simply be that they need that money for retirement. Again, there are a lot of very different situations in which it may justify someone taking those benefits at 62. According to the Social Security Administration, 72% of people take their benefits before their full retirement age. That is a very big number. What that tells me is a lot of people are not getting the advice they need to plan for Social Security to maximize their benefits.

They are giving up many benefits that could otherwise be captured to fund their retirement. Again, I think the full retirement age is very important. When you have a married couple, we typically say that the higher wage earner should wait until full retirement age to claim their benefits. That is for the benefit of themselves; it is also for the benefit of their spouse. We will get into that a little later when discussing spousal benefits. A good question I often get is, should I take my benefits at 62 versus full retirement age or wait until age 70? This is important and is something else to consider. The maximum age that you can take Social

Security is age 70. From full retirement age (FRA) to age 70, your benefits will grow by eight percent per year, including any cost of living adjustment. The benefit of waiting until you are 70 is that eight percent growth rate. If you can wait, you will maximize your benefits up until age 70. At that time, you will get the maximum amount of your benefits, getting the most out of your Social Security benefits.

Again, I want to repeat that your benefits would grow by eight percent per year from full retirement age up to 70. Even some of our best investments in the stock market today do not grow at eight percent per year plus any cost of living adjustment (COLA). Interestingly, most people do not know that the longer they wait, the more their benefit grows and the more they can spend in retirement.

Effect of late retirement on benefit (DOB: Jan. 2, 1943-Jan. 1, 1955)

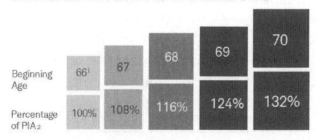

1. Represents Full Retirement Age (FRA) based on DOB Jan. 2, 1943 to Jan. 1, 1955
2. PIA = The Primary Insurance Amount is the basis for benefits that are paid to an individual

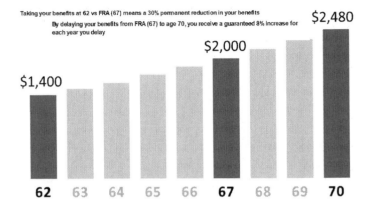

Taking your benefits at 62 vs FRA (67) means a 30% permanent reduction in your benefits

By delaying your benefits from FRA (67) to age 70, you receive a guaranteed 8% increase for each year you delay

$1,400 $2,000 $2,480

62 63 64 65 66 **67** 68 69 **70**

John's Story

For the benefit of our illustration, I will provide an example of a gentleman named John. John's story illustrates one of the negatives of taking your benefits early. John decided to start receiving his Social Security benefits at age 62, even though his full retirement age was 66. This decision had a lot of negative consequences for him. First and foremost, it reduced his monthly benefit. By claiming benefits at age 62, he received a reduced monthly benefit compared to what he would have had he waited until his full retirement age of 66. Again, that reduction is about 25% over his lifetime. That means he will receive a lower monthly benefit for the rest of his life. The result could significantly impact his financial stability in retirement or what he wants to spend. Secondly, it limits his ability to earn additional income by taking his benefits early at 62.

When most individuals claim their benefits before full retirement age, income limitations exist if they continue to work. In John's case, he wanted to continue working part-time to supplement his income, but his benefits were subject to an earnings limit. That means that if you exceed the earnings limit, Social Security will reduce your Social Security benefit by the amount you go over. Again, some of his benefits were withheld, restricting his ability to earn additional income and affecting his financial flexibility. Then the third part is that it's a missed opportunity for delayed retirement credits. As we discussed, if he had waited a little longer, he could have let those benefits grow and received much more money later. You do not have to wait until age 70, but the longer you wait, the more you will receive.

He would've been eligible for those delayed retirement credits at eight percent per year, which would have increased his monthly benefit amount. I think the point is that John missed out on the opportunity to increase his benefit through the delayed retirement credits. He took his benefits at age 62 instead of waiting until at least his full retirement age and had a lot of negative consequences because of it. He had reduced benefits, faced income limitations if he had continued working, and missed out on the opportunity to increase his benefit amount through delayed retirement credits. John and others must consider their financial situation and discuss their options with a financial professional. (It's important to note that if John changed his mind about receiving his benefits, he would have been able to withdraw his social security claim if it had been less than 12 months since he was first entitled to benefits).

It is possible to withdraw your Social Security claim if you change your mind about receiving benefits. However, there are certain conditions and requirements that you need to be aware of:

1. **Timeframe**: You can only withdraw your Social Security claim within 12 months of initially filing for benefits. This is known as the "withdrawal period."

2. **Repayment**: To withdraw your claim, you must repay all the benefits you and your family members received based on your application. This includes any spousal or dependent benefits that were paid as a result of your claim.

3. **Deadline**: You must repay the benefits within the withdrawal period, which starts from the month you initially claimed benefits. If you miss the 12-month deadline, you won't be able to withdraw your claim.

4. **One-time withdrawal**: You can only withdraw your claim for Social Security benefits once in your lifetime. If you choose to reapply for benefits in the future, you won't have the option to withdraw again.

5. **Form SSA-521**: To withdraw your claim, you need to complete Form SSA-521, officially known as the "Request for Withdrawal of Application." This form notifies the Social Security Administration (SSA) of your intention to withdraw your benefits claim.

It's important to note that withdrawing your Social Security claim and repaying the benefits can have financial implications, such as potential tax consequences or changes in future benefit amounts. It is advisable to consult with a Social Security representative or your financial advisor to fully understand the impact of withdrawing your claim before proceeding.

Chapter Three
Social Security and Spousal/Divorce Benefits

Social Security is all about maximizing what you put in, right? This is even more crucial when we are dealing with spousal benefits.

Married individuals can claim Social Security benefits based on their own personal earnings record or their spouse's earnings record when dealing with spousal benefits. They have that option; whichever one is greater. If they elect based on their spouse's earnings record, their spousal benefit could be up to 50% of their spouse's Social Security benefit. This is very important considering what we said about the 35 highest earning years. I'll use the example of my mom and my dad. When I was growing up, my dad went to work, and my mom stayed home with the kids. My dad had more earnings years than my mom. My mom had more zeros in her calculation than my dad and had a lower benefit. My mom benefitted from collecting benefits from my dad because my dad had more earnings.

Married individuals can claim their own personal or their spouse's earnings record. They cannot claim spousal benefits until their spouse files for benefits first. In the case of my mom and dad, my mom would have to wait for my dad to collect before she could collect any spousal benefits on my dad. At full retirement age, that could be up to 50% of my dad's benefits. A great example is if my dad had $2,000 a month in his benefit, and my mom wanted to take spousal benefits from my dad, she could receive up to $1,000. That $1,000 is a lot greater than what her benefit was. Combined, $1,000 plus $2000 is $3,000 a month, a lot of money over time.

I think it's important that married individuals consider their earnings record when they will claim Social Security and how that will affect their spouse and their family's total income.

What about Divorces?

In the case of divorce, it operates the same way as normal spousal benefits when you are claiming or collecting. However, in the case of divorce, there are a couple of different rules. Number one, you have to be married for at least ten years. You had to be married for at least ten years, and you had to be divorced for two years. I remember that because I always think about when we learned to drive. We had to put our hands on the wheel at ten and two. I always remembered divorce benefits the same way; 10 years married and two years divorced.

Another requirement is to be unmarried, meaning you cannot marry again (unless you are over age 60 and collecting survivor benefits). As long as you are single or unmarried, you can claim benefits from your ex-spouse. Your ex-spouse has to have qualified for Social Security. They have had to pay into Social Security and must be at least 62 years old for you to claim. But you do not have to wait for them to claim benefits for you to claim spousal benefits on your ex-spouse. You can enter Social Security and say, "I want to claim spousal benefits on my ex-spouse." You can still claim your benefits even if they have not been claimed yet. There is a very funny story related to this. About six months ago, I was working with a woman named Mary, who was 59 years old. Mary was married to a former CEO of a major tire company who made seven figures a year with very high Social Security benefits.

She was living with her boyfriend, Ed, and she approached me and said, "Are you telling me that at age 62, I can start receiving benefits from my ex-spouse?" I said, "Yes, as long as you stay single or unmarried." To which the boyfriend then said, "Well, I thought we were getting married?" And Mary said, "Not anymore!" Which was pretty funny because she understood that if she got married, she would start that 10-year clock again and could not collect from her ex-spouse. In another chapter, we will discuss survivor benefits, which apply to spousal benefits. Divorce benefits also apply to survivor benefits as well. We will touch on that a little bit.

What Many Spouses Get Wrong

There are probably a lot of different examples of things that spouses get wrong. But one example I can give you goes back to when my mom wanted to receive benefits from my dad. Remember, as long as my mom waits until her full retirement age, she will get up to 50% of my father's full retirement age benefit. I will discuss a situation where my mom might have made a mistake. Let's say, as an example, my father decided that he wanted to retire early at age 62. My father would get a reduced benefit. Again, this would correlate to a 25% reduction of Social Security benefits over your lifetime; my dad's benefits are no longer $2000 but now $1,500.

The common avoidable surprise that most couples face is that when one spouse retires at 62, the other spouse will often retire at age 62 as well and start claiming spousal benefits. If they do that, remember they do not get 50% of the full benefits. They will only get about 35% of the full spousal benefits at that point. In this situation, instead of my mom receiving $1,000 a month, my mom would only get $750 a month. Because my dad retired at 62, she decided she wanted to take spousal benefits at 62, resulting in a reduced benefit over time. What she could have done was wait until her full retirement age to collect spousal benefits. Again, my dad deciding to take his benefits at 62 is ultimately his right. But my mom is not required to take her benefits at age 62.

She could have waited until full retirement age and still received that $1,000 monthly. The common avoidable surprise couples face is not considering the income or how one spouse's decision impacts the other.

Spousal Benefits Example

I was recently working with a financial advisor and a married couple. Susan is 62, and her Full Retirement Age (FRA) is 67. Her husband, Tom, is 67 and already claiming benefits.

Susan has a Primary Insurance Amount (PIA) of $800/mo; her husband's PIA amount is $2000. Susan is eligible for up to half (50%) of his benefits or $1000 at her FRA (67). Because she worked and had her own benefits, that means Social Security would give Susan her own $800 benefit + $200 based on Tom's earnings record for a total spousal benefit of $1000 or 50% of Tom's FRA benefit of $2000.

Because Tom was already receiving his FRA benefit of $2000/mo., Susan decided she wanted to take her benefits early at age 62. I advised her that by doing so, she would get a reduction in her spousal benefits and only receive 32.5% of Tom's FRA benefit of $2000/mo. instead of the 50% amount at her Full Retirement Age (67).

By sharing several strategies with them and their advisor, I was able to save them potentially hundreds of thousands of dollars in lost spousal benefits over her life expectancy (30+ years) and help them maximize their future Social Security benefits.

Maximizing Susan's Spousal Benefits

Susan's PIA of $800/mo. is less than half ($1000) of Tom's PIA, so the most she could be eligible for is between 32.5% and 50% of Tom's PIA ($2000), depending on when she claims her benefits.

Your Spouse's Full Retirement Age Benefit Amount	Your Age	% of Your Spouse's FRA Benefit You Will Receive	Your Benefit Amount
$2,000	62	32.50%	$650
$2,000	63	35%	$700
$2,000	64	37.5%	$750
$2,000	65	41.66%	$833
$2,000	66	45.83%	$917
$2,000	67	50%	$1,000

Full Retirement Age is age 66 for those born between 1943 and 1954. Add 2 months for every year thereafter until 1960. After 1960, the FRA is age 67

Chapter Four
Social Security and Survivor Benefits

What happens when one spouse predeceases the other?

When one predeceases the other, a surviving spouse can receive or step up to the benefits of the deceased spouse. Let's return to the example of my mom and dad. My dad is receiving $2,000 a month, and my mom is getting $1000 a month. If my dad were to predecease my mom, then my mom could receive my dad's benefits of $2,000. She loses the $1,000 but steps up to the higher benefit of the $2,000. There are also some exceptions for widowers with children under 16, if you are disabled, or if you have a disabled child. Some exceptions exist to that rule where you can take survivor benefits before age 60.

Typically, survivor benefits can start as early as age 60 and not 62. However, I will tell you that if someone starts claiming survivor benefits at age 60, they are giving up about 28.5% of the survivor benefit. That is a lot of money to give up over your lifetime by taking it at 60. What I find is an avoidable surprise as it relates to taking survivor benefits in a very emotional situation where a loved one has been lost. Many widows or widowers will go into Social Security after losing their spouse, seeking to collect survivor benefits. Social Security will tell them they can start collecting at age 60. The surviving spouse does not realize or may not be told that they are giving up almost 29% of the benefit. It can be an emotional decision at the time, whereas many people need guidance and advice to avoid making the wrong decision when receiving survivor benefits.

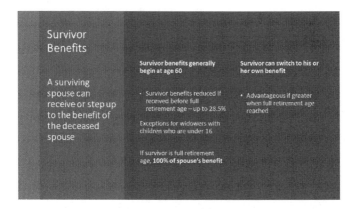

Survivor Benefits

A surviving spouse can receive or step up to the benefit of the deceased spouse

Survivor benefits generally begin at age 60

- Survivor benefits reduced if received before full retirement age – up to 28.5%

Exceptions for widowers with children who are under 16

If survivor is full retirement age, **100% of spouse's benefit**

Survivor can switch to his or her own benefit

- Advantageous if greater when full retirement age reached

What are Survivor Benefits?

People must understand what their benefits are and what their options are to maximize their benefits. For survivor benefits, we talked about possibly taking those survivor benefits at age 60, and ultimately you do have that right to do so. However, there are two other options that you can consider for widows and widowers. I will give you an example, and then we will compare the results. Let's say, as an example, I have a woman named Mary. Mary's 60, and we expect her to live to age 92. Her husband passed away this year when he was 66 years old. He had about a $2,400 benefit at age 66. Mary's own Social Security benefit at age 62 was $1,500; at age 66, it was $2,000; and at age 70, it was $2,640. I am going to give you the three options that Mary would have. She only knows and thinks she has one option: to take her survivor benefits early at age 60. That is option one.

If she does so, she receives a 28.5% reduction on her husband's $2,400. She would receive $1,716 a month starting at age 60. That is the number one strategy most people think about. The second strategy, though, which many people do not consider, is that she can start receiving that $1,716 monthly at age 60 but delay her own benefits. Remember, she has her own earnings and benefits. She can delay those benefits and receive the delayed retirement credits up to age 70. At age 70, if she switches to her benefit, her benefit becomes $2,640 monthly. Now it's important to note that taking the reduced survivor benefit initially does not affect her ability to take her benefit at a later age. That is very important, and many people do not realize she can still delay her own benefits and switch over later.

The third option is for her to begin her benefits early. Instead of taking the survivor benefits first, she could take her own benefits early at age 62. She would get $1,500 per month. Then she would switch to survivor benefits at age 66, picking up $2,400 monthly. Note that taking her benefit at age 62 does not affect or restrict her ability to take the full survivor benefit at age 66. These are important options that widows and widowers have, which is why we must sit down, discuss and compare what those options are.

Unfortunately, most people jump in and take the survivor benefits right away because they are in a situation where they feel grief, and they need a fast answer, help, and relief.

It's extremely common to take surviving benefits immediately. I would say 90% of the people that lose a loved one or lose a spouse take the survivor benefits immediately. Either because they need the income, did not receive any advice, or have not considered their other options. Remember, don't leave money on the table if you don't have to!

Social Security Survivor Benefits

I was recently working with a financial planner and his client Diane, age 60. Diane's husband Richard died recently at age 66. Diane was interested in taking her survivor benefits early at age 60 and wanted to know what her options were. Diane had a steady work history and accumulated her own benefits based on her earnings. Richard was the higher wage earner, and when he passed, his benefits were $2600/month. I informed Diane that as the surviving spouse, she could receive or step up to the benefit of the deceased spouse (Richard).

If she waited until her Full Retirement Age (FRA) of 66, she would receive 100% of Richard's benefit or $2600/month. However, if she collects survivor benefits early at age 60, Diane would only receive 71.5% of Richard's benefit or $1859/month. She would be giving up 28.5% of Richard's benefit by taking benefits early at age 60 vs waiting until age 66. By sharing several claiming strategies with Diane and her financial planner, I was able to save her almost $160,000 in lost survivor benefits over her lifetime and help her to maximize her total social security benefits.

Diane's options are below assuming a life expectancy of age 92:

Diane's Own Social Security Benefit

At age 62: $1350

At age 66: $1800

At age 70: $2232

Diane's Survivor Social Security Benefit

At age 60: $1859

At age 66: $2600

At age 70: $2600

Strategy #1
Begin survivor benefits immediately at age 60 and receive $1859/month.

Strategy #2
Begin survivor benefits immediately at age 60 and receive $1859/month, THEN, at age 70 switch over to her own benefits and receive $2232/month.
* Taking **a reduced survivor benefit** did not affect her ability to take her own benefit at a later age.

Strategy #3
Begin her own benefits at age 62 and receive $1350/month, THEN at age 66 (FRA), switch over to her survivor benefit and receive $2600/month.

* Taking her own benefit at 62 did not affect her ability to receive a full survivor benefit at **age 66**

Total Payout (Until Age 92):

Strategy #1 = $713,856
(survivor benefits only)

Strategy #2 = $812,328
($223,080 of survivor benefits + $589,248 of her own benefits)

Strategy #3 = $876,000
($64,800 of her own benefits + $811,200 of survivor benefits)

Chapter Five
Social Security and Disability Benefits

Many retirees are unaware of how Social Security and disability work together. I think there are a lot of misconceptions about Social Security and disability benefits. They are very closely related, so it is important to understand how they work. Ensuring that individuals receive the appropriate support and avoid potential risks or costs is crucial. The first thing I will tell you about disability is that there are a lot of very experienced disability attorneys out there that can help an individual with a disability. This professional is important because Social Security has a board that sits down and reviews your disability claim. They have to make sure that you have a qualifying disability. People must understand that you cannot just say you are disabled and receive disability benefits through Social Security. Every case gets reviewed through the social security review process. There are two disability programs through Social Security.

One is called Social Security Disability Insurance, otherwise known as SSDI. That provides support to individuals who have a qualifying disability.

They have worked, and they have paid into the Social Security system. As such, they are eligible for benefits.

To be eligible for Social Security Disability Insurance, you have to have a disability that prevents you from engaging in what they call substantial gainful activity. Additionally, you must have enough work credits to qualify for Social Security benefits. What we mean by substantial gainful activity is determined by the Social Security Board. You would say what your disability is, and they would review that to make sure you qualify.

The second disability benefit is Supplemental Security Income, otherwise known as SSI. That needs-based program provides financial assistance to disabled individuals with limited income and resources. These are individuals that maybe have not had a lot of earnings or have not had a very strong wage history. Unlike the first one, SSI does not require work credits but has strict income and asset limits. If you have very low wages or limited income and resources, then SSI could be a better benefit than SSDI.

SSDI vs. SSI

Social Security Disability Insurance	Supplemental Security Income
Payments come from the Social Security trust funds and are based on a person's earnings.	Payments come from the general treasury fund, NOT the Social Security trust funds. SSI payments are not based on a person's earnings.
An insurance that workers earn by paying Social Security taxes on their wages.	A needs-based public assistance program that does not require a person to have work history.
Pays benefits to disabled individuals who are unable to work, regardless of their income and resources.	Pays disabled individuals who are unable to work AND have limited income and resources.
Benefits for workers and for adults disabled since childhood. Must meet insured status requirements.	Benefits for children and adults in financial need. Must have limited income and limited resources.

Securing today and tomorrow

SocialSecurity.gov

Many people think that disability benefits come out of regular Social Security. Some people get upset when they think their Social Security is paying for disability benefits. I always try to clarify that there are two sets of disability insurance.

Social Security is Not Going Broke

We discussed the concern about Social Security going broke but did not discuss the two separate trust funds for Social Security. The individual and employer payroll tax funds the Social Security old age and survivors trust fund. The tax money collected goes directly into the old age and survivor's insurance trust fund. But there is also another trust fund called the disability insurance trust fund. That is designed to fund these disability benefits. It's important to understand that these funds are currently holding a surplus. The revenue collected from payroll taxes goes into those trust funds and then pays out those benefits accordingly, whether it's disability or retirement benefits.

Chapter Six
Social Security and Working

Many clients are unsure of retiring, so they keep working but take Social Security earlier than expected. It sometimes turns into a much bigger issue than they realize.

You can receive Social Security retirement benefits and work at the same time. However, if you are younger than your full retirement age, there can be some issues. We talked about taking your benefits early previously. We discussed that 72% of people take their benefits before full retirement age. The issues arise when you take your benefit early and make more than the yearly earnings limit. Again, I want to point out that Social Security has an earnings limit. This is also called a retirement earnings test. For 2023 the earnings limit is $21,240. When you receive benefits early and are still working, you will have a negative result if you make more than $21,240. For every two dollars you earn above the earnings limit, one dollar of your Social Security benefit will be reduced or withheld from your benefit payment.

That could be a substantial reduction over time.

The common avoidable surprise we see many people face is taking their benefits early and then going back to work to make up the difference. They do not realize that their benefits are being reduced if they make too much money. The important thing to understand here is that once you reach your full retirement age, you can make as much money as you want, and there is no limit on your earnings. By sitting down with someone and going through a plan, you can determine if taking your benefits early and working is worthwhile. Perhaps you should delay until the full retirement age and continue to work until then. At that point, there are no restrictions or no penalties.

It is an essential thing to understand. It's much more common today than it's been in years past. Especially with higher inflation and cost of living, many people return to work, whether part-time or full-time. Yet they do not understand the retirement earnings test and the limit they can have on their earnings.

Spousal Support

What about spousal support? Can collecting spousal support and then returning to work cause problems?

Yes, it can. The same retirement earnings test applies to spousal benefits as regular individual earnings. It is important to understand that it does affect you. If you were to receive spousal benefits while you are working, and you are taking your benefits early, then those benefits are affected and reduced.

It's important to note that the withheld benefits are not lost permanently. Once you reach full retirement age, the social security administration recalculates your benefits to account for the months in which benefits were withheld due to excess earnings. They will increase your monthly benefit amount to make up for the withheld benefits, and you will receive the additional amount over time. Again, you do not lose those benefits per se, but my point would be, why would you want Social Security withholding your benefits because you decided to return to work? It's important to discuss your options and maybe consider another plan or option to save you a little bit of that money.

My Neighbor John's Story

I have a great story about my neighbors, John and Amy. We sat and talked in the backyard the other day about his benefit. He worked for one of the major electric companies here and had a pretty good pension. And so, he retired early. We were talking about his retirement, and Social Security came up. He said, "Well, Amy and I have decided to take our benefit early at age 62 because we want to travel and spend some time with the grandkids. We do not want to wait to take our benefit." I said, "Well, what else is causing you to do this?" He said, "My company is hiring me back as a consultant to make about $60,000 per year." He said, "I can work part-time from my house, and they will pay me $60,000 annually. I thought that would help supplement any money we're giving up on Social Security."

I said, "Well, John, you have to understand that with this $60,000, you are well over that earnings limit. You are about $38,000 over the earnings limit ($21,240) for 2023. for every two dollars you are over, they will withhold a dollar from your benefit." If you consider the reduction, he will make $38,000 more but give up about $19,000 a year in Social Security benefits. When I told him that, he was shocked and did not realize his other options. I said, "John, if you were to work as a consultant making $60,000 a year and you wait and delay your taking of retirement benefits until age 66, then you do not have to give up all those benefits, and you get a much higher benefit." We saved him about $20,000 in lost benefits by keeping him from taking them at age 62. That is one example where we were able to help him maximize his future Social Security earnings by thinking about things a little bit differently.

If you ask John, he thought that was a lucrative lawn chair conversation! That is probably the most money he has ever made sitting in a lawn chair!

AGE	INCOME	WITHHOLDING
Under Full Retirement Age	$21,240	For every $2 over the limit, $1 is withheld from benefit
In the calendar year full retirement age is attained	$56,520	For every $3 over limit, $1 is withheld from benefit

Chapter Seven
Not Understanding How Your Benefits Might Be Taxed

I will not pay taxes on my social security.

The biggest misconception about taxes is that most people say, "Well, I have already paid taxes on my earnings when I was working. I paid the payroll tax, and I paid Medicare tax, and I paid into the system. When I start receiving Social Security, my benefits are not taxed." And that is far from the truth. According to Social Security, about 40% of people who get Social Security must pay income taxes on their benefits. I show this in several tables at the end of this chapter. There are several taxation thresholds. Your benefits may be subject to federal income tax, depending on your filing status and combined income. Several states may also tax Social Security. I believe there are 11 states that tax Social Security to some extent.

You must be living in one of these states: Colorado, Connecticut, Kansas, Minnesota, Missouri, Montana, Nebraska, New Mexico, North Dakota, Rhode Island, and Utah. They also have some form of state tax on your Social Security benefits. Other states, such as Florida and Texas, do not have a state income tax and do not impose any state tax on social security benefits. From a federal tax standpoint, the way that it works is based on your filing status. Individual filers with a combined income between $25,000 and $34,000 may have up to 50% of their benefits taxed at their ordinary income level. If individual filers have a combined income over $34,000, they could have up to 85% of their benefits taxed. Subsequently, joint filers have the same brackets. Joint filers or married couples filing jointly, with a combined income between $32,000 and $44,000, may have up to 50% of their benefits taxed.

If they have a combined income over $44,000, they may have up to 85% of their benefits taxed. I think what is important to understand is what they classify as income. From an income perspective, Social Security looks at your adjusted gross income plus any tax-exempt interest plus 50% of your Social Security benefit. This is called "provisional income." To find this amount, they take 50% of your Social Security benefit, tax-exempt interest, and adjusted gross income (everything on lines 2A and 8B of your 1040 form). Your adjusted gross income could be wages, rental income, farm income, business income, dividends, and capital gains interest, to name a few. Anything classified as income on your adjusted gross income gets added together. That is where those limits or taxation thresholds come in. Many people do not realize that in retirement, one common thing people do is start collecting all this money, not realizing the impact it will have on their social security benefits.

They collect their dividends and capital gains, and they have rental income, farm income, and all this income coming into their household for retirement. They do not realize that the income in their household is causing their taxation thresholds to increase. This, in turn, causes their Social Security benefits to be taxed. As a result, taxation takes away the income you have earned and can spend in retirement.

Provisional Income
Common Sources:

- ½ of Social Security income
- Tax-deferred distributions
- 1099 or interest from taxable accounts
- Employment income
- Rental income
- Interest from municipal bonds

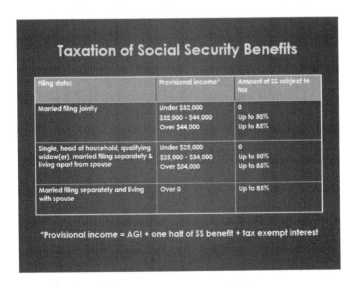

Taxation of Social Security Benefits

Filing status	Provisional income*	Amount of SS subject to tax
Married filing jointly	Under $32,000 $32,000 - $44,000 Over $44,000	0 Up to 50% Up to 85%
Single, head of household, qualifying widow(er), married filing separately & living apart from spouse	Under $25,000 $25,000 - $34,000 Over $54,000	0 Up to 50% Up to 85%
Married filing separately and living with spouse	Over 0	Up to 85%

*Provisional income = AGI + one half of SS benefit + tax exempt interest

Don't Forget to Pay Your Retirement Account Partner: the IRS

Many retirees have put much of their money into traditional accounts and left it there for retirement. When they look at their accounts, they see a lot of money accumulated to spend as future income. Unfortunately, many have not calculated that they still need to pay income taxes on that money; therefore, reducing the amount they get to spend in retirement.

Retirees start taking money from an IRA or a qualified account, including most pensions, which are all classified as income on your adjusted gross income. There are three things, though, that are not included in the income calculation that Social Security uses. Social Security uses a provisional income calculation, which I explained before. That calculation does not include any tax-deferred buildup inside IRAs, 401ks, or annuities. If your money is growing tax-deferred, earning interest and dividends, and not taking any distributions, it is not classified as income. The second thing is any income that you generate from your Roth IRAs is typically tax-free. Therefore, that income does not count as provisional income for your taxation calculation. The third thing that does not count is your life insurance policy's non-taxable income or cash value. If you were to withdraw some of your cash value from your life insurance policy and take money from your Roth IRAs, that money is not affecting your taxation on your Social Security. Minimizing the tax impact on your Social Security benefits is very important, depending on your financial situation. We highly recommend that you consult a financial planner or a tax consultant for tax advice. They can help you consider Roth conversions, tax-efficient investment strategies, and any strategies that might help you mitigate or navigate your tax impact in retirement.

More is Better… Right?

If you plan for it, that is.

I will give you a great example. Sometimes you cannot control how your income is coming in. I met an individual, a gentleman who had a very high six-figure income. He was retiring from one of the tobacco companies early and trying to think about his income situation. They were selling a couple of rental properties, and they had a business they were selling. All that income was coming into the household, including his deferred compensation payout from his company. He had no control over that payout coming to him. That deferred compensation payout would be paid to him over three years. Yet if he claims Social Security benefits, that income will hurt his ability to keep more money and force more taxation on his benefits.

Chapter Eight
Relying Solely on Social Security

The Social Security Administration has a disclaimer on their statement that says, Social Security benefits were never intended to be your only source of income when you retire. On average, Social Security only replaces about 40% of your annual pre-retirement earnings. They even state on the Social Security statement that you will need other savings, investments, pensions, and retirement accounts to have enough money to live comfortably when you retire. Social Security is telling you, do not rely on Social Security as your only source of income when you retire. In many situations, it will not be enough and will not keep up with the pace of inflation or the cost of living.

I think not considering how other sources of income affect your Social Security benefits can have several different consequences.

First, we discussed before about a reduction in benefits. Many times, the common mistake is people will take their benefits early. They will start collecting Social Security, and they know it will not be enough for retirement, so they return to work. Then they get a benefit reduction because they are above that earnings threshold. That is one example of someone not considering other sources of income when making their Social Security decision. They make a very hasty decision on Social Security, not considering the consequences. The second thing is increased taxation. Most people need to consider the other sources of income coming into their household and the impact it will have from a taxation perspective, maybe even pushing them into a higher tax bracket because they are receiving all this income in retirement.

There are ways they can reduce their overall tax situation so they do not have to owe more taxes in their retirement years when they have a very limited amount of earnings or wages to make up for that.

Many are mortified that they pay more taxes in retirement than when working. This is because they never thought about the Required Minimum Distributions (RMDs) coming into play and possibly bumping them into a higher tax bracket.

The government's been generous with us as of late. They have allowed us to delay taking our RMDs to later ages. This year you can delay your required minimum distribution to age 73. In the next couple of years, it will extend up to age 75.

So again, delaying taking some of that income has important tax implications. There are some questions you need to ask yourself. Where do you take your income first? Do you take it from your taxable account? Do you take it from your tax-free account? Do you take it from your tax-deferred account? Everyone's situation is different, but it earns the right to converse with a financial professional or planner. It is imperative to discuss what your tax impact is going to be in retirement. Because taxes are not decreasing, they are increasing over time to compensate for fewer people working in the system. The common misconception is that many people in retirement say they will pay less taxes than they did during their working years. Conversely, we do not find that to be true. We find they don't do any tax planning, and then they end up paying more in taxes in retirement than they need to.

Diversify...
But How?

If you look at the three sources of income (social security, pensions, and savings) that most people have, most people have taxable income. Fewer have pensions. Most rely on their social security benefits. They might have a brokerage account, a stock account, or mutual funds where they are subject to dividends and capital gain treatment. You can end up possibly selling your stock, receiving it, and getting capital gains treatment, which is a much lower tax rate than what your ordinary income rate might be. By taking some of that money early and letting your tax-deferred money grow, you could have more money over your lifetime. When you get closer to retirement, closer to the Social Security and Medicare age, you may want to start considering your other tax-free resources for retirement. Therefore, you will not have that tax impact on your Social Security benefits and Medicare premiums. We will talk about that in later chapters.

Retirement Today vs the Past

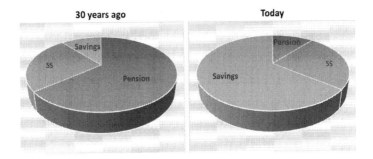

Chapter Nine
Medicare Coverage

It is hard for me to say what most people believe about Medicare. But I could tell you some common things I hear from most individuals. The number one thing most people think is that Medicare will cover all their healthcare expenses in retirement, which is simply not true. It does not cover all their expenses in retirement. It only covers about 60% of their healthcare expenses. Forty percent of that needs to be covered or paid for out of pocket. The second thing, or common misconception, is most people do not even know how much healthcare is going to cost. They think it's free. They think when they go on Medicare that, there is not going to be a cost for Medicare.

They believe there will not be an out-of-pocket cost at all or only a slight premium. That is generally not how Medicare works. If you think about when you are working and have employer coverage, your employer might pay most of that cost for your medical coverage, but you are also paying those co-pays and deductibles. Every time you go to the doctor, you pay a little out-of-pocket. It works the same way with Medicare. There are deductibles, co-pays, and coinsurance, but many individuals miscalculate how much the average cost of Medicare will be over their lifetime. I will give you an example. This is from a study through Fidelity. Fidelity estimated that an average healthy 65-year-old couple from age 65 to 85 would pay about $300,000 out-of-pocket for medical expenses over 20 years. From age 65 to 85, over $300,000 will come out of their pocket to pay for medical expenses, and this doesn't include any long-term care costs.

You say that to someone, and they do not believe you when you say that. When you break it down monthly and go through all the costs of Medicare, it does add up over time and can be quite substantial.

Big Bucks

Many people do not realize that Medicare is the second largest expense you will have in retirement, with your mortgage on your home being the largest.

Look at it this way. If somebody lives off half of their spouse's income or receives survivor benefits and their Medicare is $500 a month, that could leave them in a very difficult financial situation. With these costs and figures, they cannot live off Social Security alone.

What You Need to Know About Medicare

Here are the ABCDs of Medicare. The A stands for hospital insurance. The B stands for medical insurance. The C stands for Medicare Advantage, which we will discuss briefly. The D is drug coverage. If you think about the A, B, C, Ds of Medicare, A being hospital, B being medical, C being Medicare Advantage, and D being drug coverage, that is typically how we describe it. I will go through each one with you very simply. Part A, hospital; you have already paid this premium over your lifetime. When you pay that 1.45% Medicare tax out of your paycheck every time you are paid during your earning years, you are paying for part of Medicare. More specifically, what you are paying for is hospital coverage.

There is No Premium for Part A.

When I say that, most people say, "Well, great, it's free." Well, it's not necessarily free. It's only free if you stay out of the hospital. If you go into the hospital and/or you are admitted into the hospital, then there are deductibles and there are co-pays. It can be very, very costly. For example, if you are admitted into the hospital for inpatient treatment, Medicare Part A does cover your hospital costs once you reach your deductible, but your deductible is $1,600. You have to meet that $1,600 deductible before Medicare even starts to pay. Then there is also coinsurance. Here is a great example. For the first 60 days of your hospital stay, you are not required to pay any Part A coinsurance. However, let's say you broke your hip or your back and are in the hospital for a long time. Beginning on day 61, you must make a monthly Medicare Part A coinsurance payment of $400 through day 90.

You are paying $400 a day, every day through day 90. After day 90 in the hospital, you must pay $800 daily for up to 60 days. Beyond that, you are responsible for all the costs, and that could add up to a pretty big payment. Many people do not realize they are footing the bill when they stay in the hospital for over 90 days or more. They could come home to a bill for $11,000. They say, "Well, wait a minute. How is that possible? I did not pay any premium with Part A. Part A was supposed to be free." They do not realize that those costs do add up with hospital insurance (part A), especially if you are confined to a hospital for a long period of time.

Part B is Medical Insurance.

Part B covers any non-hospital medical coverage. It includes monthly premiums, annual deductible, coinsurance, and other potential costs. For example, I always joke, "Do you want to see, hear, eat, and walk in retirement?" What I mean by that is, typically, Medicare Part B does not cover your routine vision, dental, foot care or hearing aids. Again, there are certain things that Medicare Part B will pay for, but typically they do not cover all your vision, dental, or hearing costs. You can obtain the current "Medicare and You" brochure on our website (soosconsultinggroup.com) for more on what Medicare will cover. The part B premium in 2023 is $164.90. But what is important to understand is the Part B premium is based on your modified adjusted gross income (MAGI). They call it your modified adjusted gross income because they take all your sources of income, including your Social Security and your tax-exempt interest, minus specific deductions, and add that together.

Additionally, they do a two-year look back on your income.

What is important to understand here, and what most people do not understand, is what Medicare calls IRMAA. It stands for Income Related Monthly Adjustment Amount. There are income brackets; you can go online, and you can look at what these brackets are. For a married couple filing jointly, the income bracket starts at $194,000, and then those brackets increase as the income increases. What that means is they look at your joint tax return. If you go above $194,000, then your Medicare premiums can go higher. They do a two-year look back every year on your income. For example, if I'm turning 65 today in 2023, and I'm trying to calculate my Part B premium, Medicare is looking at my 2021 income on my tax return.

It could be possible that I was making a lot more than $194,000 two years ago. Many people do not realize this when they sign up for Medicare Part B and suddenly are paying more than $164.90 and don't understand why. Medicare can adjust your part B premium at any time during your lifetime through IRMAA. This affects widows more dramatically because the married filing joint tax table starts at $194,000, but the individual table starts at $97,000. As an example, let's say my wife and I are receiving $160,000 of total income in retirement and are not at that $194,000 threshold yet for married filing jointly. We would be paying $164.90, the minimum part B premium. So, we are paying our normal Medicare premium, and I pass away. Assuming the income we receive in retirement remains at $160,000 (MAGI) when I pass away, my wife, now a widow, is subject to the single or individual table (following the 1st year after my death). Consequently, that $160,000 of income that kept us at the lowest premium when I was alive, now pushes my wife, a widow, into the third bracket on the IRMAA table, meaning her monthly part B premium is now $428/month instead of the $164.90 we were paying.

She might not even realize why her premiums went up. She just lost her husband and now must pay more for her Medicare Part B premium, something she may or may not be able to afford.

2023 IRMAA Brackets			
2021 MAGI (single filers)	2021 MAGI (joint filers)	Part B	Part D
$97,000 or less	$194,000 or less	$164.90	Your plan premium
More than $97,000 up to $123,000	More than $194,000 up to $246,000	$230.80	$12.20 + your plan premium
More than $123,000 up to $153,000	More than $246,000 up to $306,000	$329.70	$31.50 + your plan premium
More than $153,000 up to $183,000	More than $306,000 up to $366,000	$428.60	$50.70 + your plan premium
More than $183,000 up to $500,000	More than $366,000 up to $750,000	$527.50	$70.00 + your plan premium
$500,000 or more	$750,000 or more	$560.50	$76.40 + your plan premium

For Part B, there is also a deductible of $226 per year. There are some late enrollment penalties. There are coinsurance and co-pays. And it's important to understand how that works. Then there's Part C. I will touch on C/Medicare Advantage later in this chapter.

Part D is prescription drug coverage. It's optional. You do not have to choose prescription drugs, but if you do, the premium's roughly about $32 a month. Again, that covers any of your prescription drug coverage. However, there are co-pays with Part D. For example, Medicare will pay up to a certain amount, and then you must pay out of pocket. This is commonly known as the donut hole.

You may often get additional donut hole coverage from other Medicare providers. The donut hole works because after you and Medicare spend about $4,600 in covered drugs in 2023, you enter a coverage gap called the donut hole. In this coverage gap, all your expenses are out of pocket until you reach approximately $7,400. Many people do not realize that once they pass that $4,600 threshold, everything is out of pocket until they reach $7,400. Then there is an additional co-pay that Medicare will pay after that.

Medicare Advantage Plan (Part C)

Medicare Advantage providers are dependent upon what state you live in. Medicare Advantage can be provided by Blue Cross Blue Shield, Humana, and United Healthcare, to name a few. There are a lot of different companies that provide Medicare Advantage plans. There are two ways to think about it: an unbundled plan and a bundled plan. Unbundled is traditional Medicare coverage. Seventy-five percent of people choose original Medicare, which means it's kind of like a la carte. They choose Part A and Part B, and then they pay the premium. They can have drug coverage, which is optional. Maybe they buy a Medigap policy to cover some of the gaps in their coverage. Traditionally that is what most people do. That is a typical unbundled plan, and you pay a premium for that. A typical married couple can be expected to pay anywhere between $12,000 and $14,000 per year out-of-pocket.

Remember, you have out-of-pocket costs that Medicare does not cover. That could cost you between $12,000 to $14,000, about $7,000 each, out-of-pocket. Traditional Medicare costs anywhere between $5,000 to $7,000 for each person. The bundled plan in Medicare Advantage means bundling all your parts together. They will bundle Part A, B, and in most cases, D (drug coverage). Many Medicare Advantage plans, called all-in-one or bundled plans, will mean you pay one premium for all that coverage.

Most Medicare Advantage plans offer coverage for things that aren't covered by Original Medicare, like vision, dental, hearing and wellness programs (like gym memberships). In most cases, you'll need to stay within their network of doctors. However, many plans offer out-of-network coverage, but sometimes at a higher cost. For example, you may have an issue with this because you have a heart problem. You always went to the same heart doctor who, unfortunately, is not within the network of doctors in your Medicare Advantage plan. Your options would be to switch to another heart doctor within the plan because of availability or go out-of-network and potentially pay a much higher premium or cost. There are many aspects of Medicare that you need to know to understand it fully, but hopefully, this has covered most of those parts.

Many people do not realize there may be consequences if they leave regular Medicare and go to Medicare Advantage. For example, if they do not like it and want to return, they will be charged current pricing for Medicare versus their previous rate.

That said, they can switch back and forth from Medicare to Medicare Advantage and vice versa during the open enrollment period. Every year there is an enrollment period, typically from October 15th to December 7th. Typically, you can switch back and forth if you want to. But again, you are subject to whatever those premiums are at that time.

The A-B-Cs of Medicare

Part A covers inpatient hospital stays, skilled nursing facility stays, some home health visits, and hospice care.

Part B covers physician visits, outpatient services, preventive services, and some home health visits.

Part C refers to the Medicare Advantage program through which beneficiaries can enroll in a private health plan.

Part D covers outpatient prescription drugs through private plans that contract with Medicare.

Chapter Ten
Medicare Costs

There are five avoidable surprises most people make with Medicare costs.

Number one is not sign signing up for Medicare on time. One avoidable surprise people make is missing their enrollment window. Your enrollment window is seven months, starting three months before your 65th birthday, the month of your birthday, and the three months after your 65th birthday. Make sure that you understand when that signup window is. If someone is eligible for Medicare and doesn't sign up during their initial enrollment period, they may have to pay a penalty for late enrollment. This penalty can be significant and last for the rest of their life. Therefore, be careful about not missing that enrollment period. The second part is what we discussed earlier, not understanding or educating themselves on the different parts of Medicare.

Many people do not understand the difference between these parts and how each part works. They may end up with gaps in their coverage or pay for services they do not need.

Additionally, not reviewing your plan annually is another avoidable surprise. We discussed reviewing your Social Security, but you must also review your Medicare plan. Plans and costs can change from year to year. It's important to review because you may not have the same needs today that you will have 20 years from now. Some people don't review their plans and may miss out on new benefits or end up with a plan that no longer meets their needs. Another major issue or concern is not planning for or understanding the costs of Medicare. There are premiums, deductibles, and coinsurance. It's amazing how many people do not understand these costs and are surprised by how much they must pay for healthcare services in retirement. So please make sure you plan early and often. Finally, the last avoidable surprise is not reporting your changes in income.

Medicare premiums, again, are based on income. People that do not report the changes in their income to Social Security can have incorrect premiums and penalties for not reporting the changes.

For example, in many cases, selling rental or primary property is not classified as income for Social Security benefits. However, if you sell your home for taxable income and make a hefty profit, there may be an increase in your Part B or D premiums for Medicare. Some of that income may be exempt from your income calculation, so it is important to understand how that income is calculated.

Properly reporting your income on your tax return and to Social Security and Medicare will ensure that you are paying accurate premiums. If you receive benefits from Social Security, you have a legal obligation to report changes that could affect your eligibility for disability, retirement, and supplemental security income (SSI) benefits. If you fail to report changes in a timely way or if you intentionally make a false statement, Social Security may stop your SSI, disability, and retirement benefits. They may also impose a sanction against your benefits which could mean a loss of payments for 6, 12, or as long as 24 months.

Medicare Cost Comparison, Year-Over-Year

	2022	2023
Part A Premium	$499	$506
Part A Deductible	$1,556	$1,600
Part A Daily Co-Pay: Days 61-90	$389	$400
Part A Daily Co-Pay: Days 91-150	$778	$800
Part A Skilled Nursing Co-Pay	$194.50	$200
Part B Premium	$170.10	$164.90
Part B Deductible	$233	$226
Part B Co-Insurance	20%	20%

What if Social Security and Medicare are Not Done Correctly?

Your Part B medical insurance premium is automatically deducted from your Social Security check when collecting Social Security. Many people do not realize they are automatically reducing their social security check every month by their part B premium. The issue can compound itself in several ways. First, if your part B premium is increased due to IRMAA with the two-year look back provision, more money gets deducted from your social security check. Secondly, if you decided to collect your Social Security early with a reduced benefit, and Medicare is now reducing your monthly payment, we call that a double negative. It's a double negative because you took your benefits early on Social Security, collecting a smaller check, then Medicare reduces it further by deducting the Part B premium giving you less money to spend in retirement.

Social Security and Medicare go hand in hand. If you can maximize your Social Security benefits, it allows you the ability to pay your Medicare premiums and for those unexpected medical costs over time.

Medicare Misbeliefs

I think very important to note that long-term care and Medicare are separate entities. They serve very different purposes in healthcare. Long-term care is a plan designed to assist individuals with activities of daily living. What we mean by activities of daily living are bathing, dressing, eating, toileting, medication management, and other activities. Those services typically are not covered by traditional insurance or Medicare but can be expensive as we age. Many older couples are going through that right now. Individuals needing long-term care service either pay out-of-pocket, rely on long-term care insurance if they qualify for that, or Medicaid. But to qualify for Medicaid, they must meet certain income and asset requirement specifics.

Typically, if someone has a chronic illness, disability, or cognitive impairment, they need long-term care services. My friend's father has Parkinson's and heart issues. Individuals like him need the care, either through in-home or through an assisted living facility. What is very important is there are several different ways that you can get long-term care. One is through a skilled nursing facility. Part A of Medicare only covers a limited amount of skilled nursing care in a skilled nursing facility and under specific conditions. To be eligible, a person has to have a qualified hospital stay, similar to Part A.

Additionally, the hospital stay must be related to the condition they are hospitalized for. They will cover the first 20 days at 100%, so no cost goes to the client. But from day 21 to day 100, the individual is responsible for coinsurance. After day 100, Medicare coverage ends.

If the person is still at a skilled nursing facility after 100 days, they pay all costs out of pocket. Medicare does not pay anything after day 100. This gets you thinking about how all these costs can add up, especially as we age. The second major cost is home healthcare. People typically do not want to be in a facility, so they want to have their care at home. Part A and Part B will cover certain home healthcare services, part-time or intermittently, but not full-time. I will give you an example. Some services provided are skilled nursing care, physical therapy, occupational therapy, and speech therapy. Any of those things are considered home healthcare. The person has to be homebound and has to require skilled care. Medicare will cover 100% of the approved amount for home health services. Medicare Part A and B will also provide some of the cost for hospice care.

For anyone who is terminally ill, Medicare will cover some nursing care, hospice aids, social worker services, and more. However, they will not cover some of the medical treatments. They will not cover any room and board, medical treatment, medication, or anything similar to that if someone is in hospice. Here are some current costs for these services. The current cost for a private nursing home room is $9,034 per month. That is over $108,000 per year for a private nursing home room; in many cases, that does not cover any food, beverages, or other amenities. If you were required to have a private room in an assisted living facility, those costs would be approximately $4,500 a month or about $54,000 a year.

A home health aide can be very expensive and typically is not full-time coverage. Home health care costs about $5,148 a month or about $61,000 a year. The biggest concern we see is as we age, the more help we need, the more medical care we need, and the more costly it becomes. The Center for Longevity estimated that an average 65-year-old married couple today will have a 50% chance that one of them will live to age 92. There is a 25% chance one of them will live to age 98. It's a good news, bad news story. The good news is we're living longer; the bad news is we're living longer.

Women Live Longer

A note, on average, women tend to live longer than men. Women have a life expectancy of 79 years, while men have a life expectancy of 73 years. Over seventy percent of all residents in nursing homes or assisted living facilities are women. In many cases, it's the ladies that are going to outlive the men. It's imperative, especially with married couples, to have a thorough discussion and plan collectively to ensure that these medical and long-term care costs are covered.

Chapter Eleven
Here is How We Can Help You Help Your Clients

Hopefully, you enjoyed this book and benefitted from the strategies discussed. If you did, please kindly leave a review on Amazon, Kindle Books or Google. I would encourage you to schedule a strategy or discovery session with me. This first meeting is the time for me to understand the financial advisor's practice, their business, their clients, and their needs and objectives to discover what you need to know about Social Security and Medicare. It also helps me determine whether you need my services and what resources I can provide. Depending on the conversation, this meeting could last 30 to 40 minutes or slightly longer.

By the End of the Meeting

By the end of the meeting, I will have a better understanding of the financial advisor and their clients' needs. Specifically, I will better understand their comfort level with Social Security and Medicare. What I wish to discover by the end of that meeting is a greater understanding of their knowledge level, what they know about the numerous Social Security claiming strategies, details of Medicare, and how I can help them help their clients. I have a phrase that I live by in my practice: <u>Education without implementation is just entertainment</u>.

What I mean by that is that if you just read my book and take no action, the book has only entertained you for the time it took for you to read it. However, if you can implement one strategy, one practice, and one benefit from either reading my book or working with me, then I'm confident together, we can help you educate your clients, helping them live a happier, more fulfilled retirement with fewer worries. Why is that important?

Having happier and more financially educated clients can have a significant positive impact on their lives in several ways:

1. **Improved Financial Well-being**: Financial education can help clients better understand their finances, make informed decisions, and manage their money effectively. This can lead to improved financial well-being, reduced financial stress, and increased financial security.
2. **Better Retirement Planning**: A financially educated client is more likely to have a well-planned retirement strategy, including a solid understanding of Social Security and Medicare benefits. This can help them achieve their retirement goals and enjoy a comfortable retirement.
3. **Increased Confidence**: Clients who are more financially educated are likely to feel more confident and empowered when it comes to managing their finances. This can lead to better decision-making, increased financial independence, and a greater sense of control over their financial future.
4. **Better Quality of Life**: Improved financial well-being and increased confidence can lead to a better quality of life overall. Clients may have more opportunities to pursue their passions, travel, and enjoy their retirement years without worrying about financial constraints.

Overall, having happier and more financially educated clients can lead to a more fulfilling and enjoyable life, with greater financial security and peace of mind.

How to Get in Touch

Contact me at my website, which is **www.soosconsultinggroup.com**. You can also reach me through email with any questions or inquiries at: **msoos@soosconsultinggroup.com.** On my website, there is a section to book a strategy session/consulting appointment. You can go there, read a little about our services and what we provide, and then book an appointment. Also, on my website, please click on the "Let's Chat!" button to ask any questions you have on Social Security or Medicare. I'm always available to help! I'm planning to do several local workshops in the North Carolina area, as well as in other states. I will advertise those from time to time on my website. Hopefully, financial advisors can come out and learn a little more about Social Security and Medicare.

Chapter Twelve
About the Author

 Michael Soos is a distinguished professional and the President/Founder of Soos Consulting Group, a highly regarded business consulting firm. With an illustrious career spanning over 34 years in the financial services industry, he has made significant contributions while working with a leading Fortune 500 company.

Throughout his tenure, Michael has demonstrated an unwavering dedication to assisting financial professionals and their clients in crafting comprehensive retirement plans. Possessing a wealth of expertise in Social Security and Medicare, Michael is recognized as a subject matter expert. His profound knowledge and insights make him an invaluable resource for financial advisors, CPAs and attorneys seeking solutions for their clients' income planning needs. By sharing proven business strategies and offering education on industry-related changes, he empowers these professionals to enhance their practices and serve their clients more effectively. As a testament to his commitment to knowledge dissemination, Michael has conducted over 2000 workshops and lectures on Social Security and Medicare. Additionally, he has been a Continuing Education Instructor for more than 26 years. He graduated from St. John's University, where he earned a bachelor's degree in business management.

Residing in Mooresville, North Carolina, Michael cherishes his time with his wife, Noreen, and their adopted children, Katrina, Matthew, and Gabriella. Outside of his professional endeavors, he enjoys competitive powerlifting, traveling with his family, and indulging in the game of golf.

Soos Consulting Group was created to provide financial advisors with a comprehensive overview of Social Security and Medicare and how they impact retirement planning. It provides practical guidance and strategies for helping clients make informed decisions about their benefits and coverage.

Navigating Social Security isn't as straightforward as you might think. Maximizing, or at least preserving your benefit amount takes forethought, planning, and oftentimes collaboration. It's not just a matter of claiming your benefits and collecting a check. There's actually a lot of strategy that goes into effectively managing Social Security income. Understanding how to implement successful claiming strategies will help your clients avoid leaving money on the table and keep more of what they deserve.

Additionally, managing Medicare costs can be complex and confusing at times. Learning the important ins and outs of Social Security and managing healthcare costs are a few elements of preparing for a successful retirement.

Speak with us today and see how we can help!

Chapter Thirteen
Testimonials

As a CFP and 24-year veteran of the financial services industry, I am blown away by Michael's knowledge of the intricacies surrounding Social Security and Medicare. He has helped many clients strategize to maximize payouts and optimize these government benefits. My wife Sarah, an attorney, works with me in the business. Likewise, she admires Michael's ability to apply careful analysis to solve complex client needs.

Geoff Kemble, CFP, CLTC
Kemble Financial
Matthews, NC

Dr. Soos is the man! I met Michael Soos when his former company hired me to speak to financial advisors. I watched and listened several times as Michael presented information and strategies to advisors and their clients on Social Security and Medicare. I recently had him on my podcast; as of today, it is one of the most talked about podcasts I have done. The man knows his stuff. He has made it his purpose in life to help others on these topics and can help you. He has helped me!

Steve Beecham
Home Town Mortgage
Alpharetta, GA

I have worked with Michael Soos for many years and have been very impressed with his knowledge and passion for Advisors and Clients. He has helped countless advisors bring a more professional process to their work with clients. His thirst to help people maximize their retirement is infectious. This book is a must-read.

Kevin P. Taylor
Director of Firm Business Development
Strategic Planning Group
Atlanta, GA

*Michael is my go-to person when needing
Social Security and Medicare benefits expertise.
His vast knowledge has helped several of my
financial planning clients. In addition, he has
been a guest speaker at my Advisor Forum,
providing continuing education credits for
CPAs, Financial Advisors, and Attorneys. He
has been ranked the #1 speaker several years in
a row. Michael is a man of honesty and
integrity. He is willing to go above and beyond
expectations.*

Jeff Palmer
Financial Planner
The Palmer Group
Asheville, NC

Maximizing Social Security and Medicare Benefits for Your Clients

As you know, Social Security benefits are a critical source of income for many retirees. Mixing that with a lack of planning and clients making decisions by themselves about Medicare selection and funding can put them at risk of over-taxation and loss of benefits.

Recent research shows that despite the glaring need for Social Security and Medicare advice, many financial advisors and their clients are not completely comfortable or informed of the numerous Social Security and Medicare concepts and strategies:

- A 2019 study by the **Nationwide Retirement Institute** found only 17% of financial advisors felt very confident in their knowledge of *Social Security benefits.*

- A 2018 survey by the **National Association of Personal Financial Advisors (NAPFA)** found that only 10% of financial advisors felt very confident in their knowledge of *Medicare.*

- A 2017 survey by the **American College of Financial Services** found only 17% of financial advisors felt very confident in their knowledge of *Social Security claiming strategies.*

These studies suggest that there are many financial advisors who need advice and mentoring to provide practical guidance and strategies to help their clients make informed decisions about their benefits and coverage. That's where I come in. I help financial advisors just like you every day.

To learn more about the ideas discussed in this book, here's what you do next:

Step 1: Go to **www.soosconsultinggroup.com** and book an appointment or email me directly at **msoos@soosconsultinggroup.com** then;

Step 2: We will spend 30-45 minutes with you during a ***Solutions Strategy Session*** to identify your and your clients' needs, specifically around Social Security and Medicare.

Step 3: Provide a list of resources and services we provide to help you and your practice outlining specific strategies/solutions to address your concerns. We can also Book a separate **Solutions Strategy Session** where we sit with you during your client meeting to identify your client's needs around Social Security and Medicare.

I look forward to helping you help your clients keep more of their Social Security and Medicare Benefits.